**Olaru Constan**

# BUCHAREST CITY GUIDE

Descrierea CIP a Bibliotecii Naționale a României
OLARU, CONSTANTIN
  Bucharest City Guide / Olaru Constantin. – București: Editura
My Ebook, 2016
  ISBN 978-606-8846-62-0

Olaru Constantin

# BUCHAREST CITY GUIDE

My Ebook Publishing House
Bucharest, 2016

# TABLE OF CONTENTS

# I. A City of Boulevards and Parks

The capital of Romania, the cultural and economical center of the entire country, was established more than five hundred years ago and it is the most suitable starting point for a tour of Romania. In the years thirty, Bucharest was surnamed "Small Paris" because of its boulevards guarded by trees.

Here even a Triumph Arch is found, on the impressive Kisseleff driveway which is longer than Champs Elyse and on which, during spring, you can admire the splendor of the blooming trees. Despite the extended plan of reconstruction from the eighties, Bucharest remains a city of parks, pleasant, full of grass, with coffee-shops open on the sidewalks during the summer and pleasure boats on the lakes and rivers that cross it.

## Exploring the City

It is easy to get around in Bucharest. The subway network extends on the whole surface of the town, and the price for a trip is unique. The main boulevards cross the town on the direction north-south, from the Triumph Arch until the Civic Center, and are intersected by others that spread from east to west. The victory Path, which is found in the following of the Kisseleff driveway, is the favorite place by the inhabitants of the capital city for walks in the summer evenings.

Here you will find imposing public buildings, such as The National History Museum and the Post Palace, and toward the southern end of this boulevard lays the Cismigiu Garden. The Magheru Boulevard is parallel with Victory Path, and on it are found tourism agencies and airway company agencies, cinemas and hotels.

## An Eclectic Combination of Stiles

You will probably be surprised by the eclectic mix of architectural styles from Bucharest starting from The Old Court, the remaining of the palace from the fifteenth century of Vlad Tepes- the one that founded the city and, at the same time, the inspiration source for the character Dracula-, to orthodox churches, at mansions in the Second Empire style, at the heavy Stalinist architecture from the communist period and finishing with the Palace of Parliament, a colossal building with six thousand rooms, the second as size in the world after The Pentagon. In Bucharest, there are always especially interesting things which are waiting to be discovered.

**What Is Worth Visiting**

It is worth visiting Bucharest, if only for its museums, especially the Village Museum outdoor that is found in The Herastrau Park, along The Triumph Arch. Here you will see examples of the popular architecture and handicrafts from the entire Romania, including the famous wooden small churches from Maramures. Other "mandatory" objectives are The National Museum of Art, which is found in the building of the ex Royal Palace, The National History Museum from the Victory Path, which accommodates the gorgeous silverware of the national treasure, and The Old Court, with its painted little church from the sixteenth century.

Close by lies the splendid Patriarchal Church, built in 1657, which now represents a contrasting note up against the modernity of the entire Civic Center. And do not miss the Stavropoleos church next the Old Court, a true jewelry of the Romanian orthodox architecture. If you are lucky to be standing in one of these churches during a baptism or a wedding, you will assist to a ceremony that you will never forget.

### The Bohemian Life In Bucharest

The artistic life of the city was always at the height of its Parisian nickname, and today it is more active than ever. The national opera always keeps a classic repertoire- Puccini, Verdi, Rossini, and Mozart.

In the splendid building in neo-classic style of the Romanian Athenaeum take place international concerts or performed by the Philharmonic Orchestra George Enescu. Still, the price of the tickets is way smaller than in other countries.

### What Can the City Center Offer You

All the tourists like to shop; you will find stores in the area of the Union Square and on the main boulevards. To make a change, you can walk into a bazaar with small merchants on the small roads from the area of the Lipscani Street, close to the Old Court. The objects with local specific are the ceramic, glassware, fabrics and wooden sculptures.

Another memorable experience would be to visit the agitated Rag Fair of Sunday morning, meaning a junk market on the shore of Dambovita. The restaurants of the capital city have come alive again; the roast beef, chicken or pig are found at the base of many typical dishes and are followed by a various range of pastry specialties at desert. For a better appetite, taste the Romanian wines and tuica, the national drink.

The prices are reasonable and the atmosphere from the bars, restaurants and nightclubs is welcoming, most of the times cheered by the rhythms of gipsy music. The Romanians are a people full of live which like to enjoy themselves. Join them and have fun!

## The Surroundings of the Capital City

Bucharest is surrounded by woods and lakes, and old palaces and monasteries are found in this picturesque scenery. The monastery with a steeple from Snagov, which dates from 1408, is very prized by the people from Bucharest which practice nautical sports on the lake.

It is worth visiting the elegant Mogosoaia Palace, built in the eighteenth century, which is found at a distance of fourteen kilometers (nine miles) north of Mogosoaia Lake. There are though many other places that are worth visiting.

# II. The tour of the Bucharest

Even though it had a lot to suffer along the time, invasions, fires, inundations, earthquakes, the rage of an insane dictator and newer, but maybe the most serious the indifference of everyone, Bucharest has things to show to the visitor either he is coming from the province or from abroad. It would a waste to pass through Bucharest without seeing at least a part of what we propose in the following.

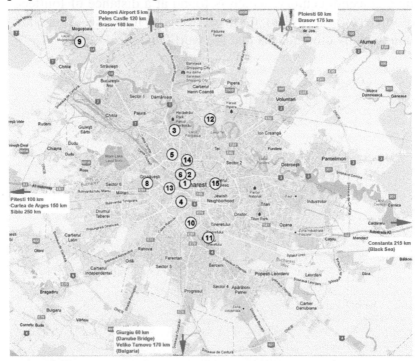

**Map Legend:**

1. Old City Center; 2. Romanian Atheneum; 3. Village Museum; 4. "House of the People" / Palace of Parliament; 5. Natural Sciences Museum "Grigore Antipa"; 6. National History Museum; 7. National Art Museum; 8. Cotroceni Palace; 9. Mogosoaia Palace; 10. Technical Museum in Carol Park; 11. Tineretului Park; 12. Aviation Museum; 13. Cișmigiu Gardens; 14. Astronomic Observatory

# The Athenaeum

C. Esarcu, V. A. Ureche and N. Kretulescu established in 1865 the institution The Athenaeum with the purpose of "gifting the people with useful knowledge". To raise the money necessary for the construction of the building it was called to the public collection having the motto "Give a leu for the Athenaeum".

In 1886 started the construction according to the plans of the French architect Albert Galleron and was inaugurated at 14 of February 1888. Here has the headquarters the "G. Enescu" philharmonic orchestra and also here evolved some of the most famous conductors and soloist performers of the twentieth century: Erich Kleiber, Sergiu Celibadache, Ionel Perlea, Herbert von Karajan, Dinu Lipatti, Arthur Rubinstein, Pablo Casals, Yehudi Menuhin.

## The Basarab Bridge

Saturday,! It inaugurated in … Romania!!! Yes, we know that it seems a statement of science-fiction domain, but happily it is true. The Basarab passageway from Bucharest, is the widest urban bridge from Europe (forty four meters) and links the Nicolae Titulescu driveway and the Grozavesti driveway, it is a true architectural wonder… It is great and impressive.

## The National Opera Bucharest

Even though in Romania manifestations of the lyrical genre date since the nineteenth century, the building of the Romanian Opera is a construction relatively new (1953) built according to the plans of the architect Octav Doicescu.

It has a capacity of two thousand and two hundred seats, also it hosts at the last flour The Opera Museum in which are exposed documents, photographs, costumes illustrating the development of this artistic genre in Romania. In front of the building lies the statue of the great musician George Enescu, a bronze sculpture by Ion Jalea.

## The National Arena

With a capacity of fifty five thousands six hundred spectators, the National Arena is the biggest stadium from the country and the first elite UEFA stadium in Romania. The stadium has a surface of one hundred and eight thousand square meters and a height of six flours.

The construction includes a subterranean garage with two hundred parking seats, forty boxes of twelve seats each, conference rooms and restaurants. Also, the stadium has ninety four access ways, which allows that the evacuation of the spectators to be made in twenty minutes. The arena is also tooled up with a video cube, situated above the center of the field, equipped with four screens of thirty square meters each.

## The Cretulescu Church

The Cretulescu Church, known also under the name Kretzulescu church is an orthodox place of worship from Bucharest. Considered one of the most valuable monuments of architecture of the city from the end of the brancovenian period, the Cretulescu church was built in the years 1720-1722 by the care of the great chancellor Iordache Cretulescu and his wife Safta, one of the daughters of the ruler Constantin Brancoveanu.

The great chancellor built in the vicinity of the church an inn as well, not only because it was customary in those days, but also because of the fact that here was found, at that time, the northern barrier of the city, on the "great road" or "The Mogosoaia bridge", in the place called at that time "The mail well".

The construction has a trefoil plan, carrying above the nave a slender steeple, and above the narthex, the belfry. Both are equipped with narrow and long windows, accentuating the tendency of verticality of the monument, which is realized through the decorative plastic of the facades. These are separated in two floors, the inferior one being decorated with rectangular panels, and the superior one with double arches, prolonged.

The entrance into the church is made through an open threshold, supported on tall columns of stone between which open simple arcades in full center. The exterior of the church was mortared at the origin but with the occasion of the restoration made in the years 1935-1936, under the care of the architect Stefan Bals, it remained in apparent brick. The painting in the threshold is the original one, and the one from the inside belongs to Gheorghe Tattarescu, being realized between the years 1859-1860.

The church was repaired also between the years 1942-1943, because of the earthquake from 1940. In the communist period it was expected that the Kretzulescu church was going to be demolished. It was saved because of the architects, among which we remind madam Henriette Delavrancea. It was realized a new restoration both at the exterior as at the interior, after the earthquake from 1977 as well after the revolution from 1989. All these works have been realized with the support of the parochial priest Vasile Raduca. The restoration started in 1996 and lasted until 2003, when the old painting has been partially washed.

# The Cismigiu Garden

On the place of the actual park, in the times of Alexandru Ipsilanti was found a great slop, called the slop of Dura the merchant. The actual name was gained from the chief over the fountains which had the house close by. In 1847, under the guidance of the Viennese landscaper Carl F. W. Meyer, have started the works of arranging, and in the year 1854 took place the official inauguration.

The garden impresses even today through the floral arrangements, the great collection of arboretum material, here being found some trees declared protected. The Cismigiu is never deserted, in the summer being appreciated for the chill, vegetation and its lake full of boats and which at winter becomes a natural rink.

# The Royal Palace

The royal palace is a monumental building from Bucharest, initially a center of the monarchic power in Romania. In the present it is the National Museum of Art of Romania headquarter. In 1837, the sumptuous house of the steward Dinicu Golescu built in this place becomes the Royal Court of Lord Alexandru Ghica.

From 1859 until 1866 here lived the ruler of the United Princedom, Alexandru Ioan Cuza. From 10 may 1866 the house becomes the residence of the ruler Carol the first. After the fire from 1826 which destroyed the central body, it becomes necessary its replacement. In 1935-1936 the old house is demolished.

The palace was built according to the plans of the architect Nicolae Nenciulescu and finished in the year 1937. The construction is in the shape of U, with an interior yard. The frontage has two entrances: the left entrance was used by the king and his guests and the one from the right was destined for the officials. To the left, the entrance leads into an octagonal lobby, decorated in neo-byzantine style where the staircase of the guests climbs and to the right, it is entered into the official lobby, a great square hallway, where the staircase of the rulers climbs toward the ex throne room. During the Revolution from 1989, the palace was set afire.

## The Old City Center

The Old City Center represents one of the important objectives of the entertainment tourism from Bucharest. It is a zone full of bars, pubs, a lot of beer and a core of the night life from Bucharest.

# The National Military Circle

The building of the National Military Circle was built in the year 1912 according to the plans of the architects D. Maimaroiu, V. Stefanescu and E. Doneaud, being tributary to the French neoclassic style. It has sumptuous interiors which hosted along the time balls, reunions and nowadays, painting exhibitions, sculptures, book launches, etcetera.

Even though this place has an interesting history, few people know it. The first clue is the fountain from the front of the National Military Circle which is called Sarindar, after the name of the church probably built by Matei Basarab, much later, at the end of the eighteenth century, which was famous for the painting of the Virgin Mary, miracles accomplisher. Rebuilt many times, the church was gravely affected by the earthquake from 1838, ruining then slowly.

# The Economies and Consignments House

The Economies and Consignments House as an institution was established in the year 1864 through a law initiated by Alexandru Ioan Cuza. In the beginning it worked in various buildings, after which in the year 1875 it was started building their own headquarter. On the spot where the Economies and Consignments House lies today was found then the Saint John the Great church which was demolished to make room for the first construction.

The Economies and Consignments House develops fast so that the old headquarter becomes too small, so it is decided the demolition of the old headquarter and on the same spot it was started building the actual headquarter, according to the plans of the French architect Paul Gottereau. The start of the works was marked through a ceremony that took place at 8 june 1897, amongst the participants being the royal family, members of the government, members of the administration board of the Economies and Consignments House, the architect Paul Gottereau. The construction was finished in the year 1900 and since then the Economies and Consignments House functioned in this building without being made other notable modifications.

## The Geology Museum

    The National Geological Museum is a museum from Bucharest situated on the Kisseleff driveway, close by the Victory Square and the Kisseleff Park. In the year 1990 was opened for the public, in the building of the Geological Institute of Romania, built in 1906. The permanent exhibition is formed of fourteen basic exhibitions and contains over eighty thousand samples found in the scientific collections of the museum.

# The Stavropoleos Church

Hidden amongst higher buildings, the Stavropoleos Church is found behind the ex Post Palace (the actual National History Museum). The small and very beautiful church was built by a Greek monk established on our lands, on his name Ioanichie. It is a sanctuary with the most representative and excellent influences of the late brancovenian art.

The rock columns, the pedestals, the gorgerins, the threshold with a banister delight the eye through the craftsmanship of the sculptures with vegetal motifs or animals. The earthquakes along the years, but most of all, "the big one" from 1802 and then the one from 1838 caused it great damages, even demolishing the steeple from on top of the nave. The restoration starts only at about 1900, under the command of the architect Ion Mincu, which worked diligently until the year of his death, 1912; the finalization of the work is made by one of his students, the architect Alexandru Zagoritz.

## The National History Museum

The National History Museum of Romania, arranged in the ex Post Palace, building built in the neo-classic style. It is the most important museum of the Romanian state. It owns objects with historical value discovered on the actual territory of Romania, from prehistoric times and up to the contemporary period.

The collections of the museum contain approximately seven hundred thousand objects: fossils, jewelries, tools, weapons from the history of the Romanians, historical documents and ornaments, numismatics and thesaurus. Permanently, the collections of the museum are enriched through donations, acquisitions and new archeological discoveries.

# The Manuc Inn

In the old market of Bucharest, starting from about 1700, existed a few tenths of inns, each one more picturesque than the other, which have known a true glory age, for almost two hundred of years.

According to the origin or the social status of the founder and according to the specific of these commercial institutions, the Bucharest's inns from old have been called "princely", "monastic" or "clerical", "lordly" and "mercantile", therefore all of them had the same economical purpose, amongst the old market. In the last category the historians also placed "Manuc's Inn", from afar one of the most famous constructions of this type from Valahia, not only because of its imposing sizes, but also through the figure of its builder, the legendary "Manuc Bey". There it is, shortly, the story of the controversial historical character and of the inn which carries his name up until today.

# The Grigore Antipa Museum

The National Natural History Museum "Grigore Antipa" has its origin in the National Natural History and Antiques Museum from Bucharest, founded at 3 November 1834 through the act 142 signed by the prince Alexandru Ghica. The initiative belonged to the great lord Mihalache Ghica, minister of "Inside Affaires" and the brother of the ruler prince which was also the first donor of the museum. It works into a building built in the period 1904-1908 at the initiative of Grigore Antipa.

The museum captures the dynamic of the life on earth from the moment of its apparition until the level of the contemporary man, and has a rich patrimony formed of zoological collections, minerals and rocks, paleontological and ethnographic. As a consequence of the collecting realized by specialists from the country and abroad, of the donations and acquisitions, the collections of the museum increased permanently, such as, in the present, they contain over two million pieces. This year, the museum reopened its gates after two years and a half of works at the permanent exhibition.

## The Palace of Parliament

The Palace of Parliament, known before the Revolution from 1989 under the name of the House of the Republic or the House of People, was built between the years 1984 and 1989 and it is the second greatest building from the world as surface, after the Pentagon. It has eighty four meters in height, twelve floors and six thousand rooms.

On the inside it is decorated with Romanian marble and walnut and sour cherry wood. In the shape of a pyramid without a top, the palace contains vast hallways, long corridors, numerous immense rooms, and the biggest is called the Union Hall, which has a height of sixteen meters and a surface of two thousand and two hundred square meters. In this building Nicolae Ceausescu wanted to be the residence of the presidency, of the Central Comity of the Communist Party and of the ministries. For raising it, there were demolished entire districts, on a surface of over seven square kilometers from the old center of Bucharest.

Over forty thousand people had to leave that area. There have been demolished churches and buildings that had a patrimonial value. It is not known exactly the number of those that died during the construction of the House of the People, but at its building worked, in very hard conditions, workers and soldiers brought from all over the country.

The interiors restore the opulence of which was marked the former dictator: immense marble stairs, ceilings with laces of ornaments, mosaics, richly sculptured doors, entire rows of chandeliers-some even having seven hundred bulbs, rugs executed on special orders.

The House of People was built on the former Spirii Hill (the name of a renowned doctor from the area) after the eighties, when the "urbanisation" of the entire neighborhood began, at the "indications of the genius founder". Raised on an artificial hill, the House of People has a height of eighty four meters, (it contains twelve flours) has a dominant note, imposing, and with its surface of three hundred and thirty thousand square meters, it becomes the second building in the world after the Pentagon.

Here Ceausescu wanted to be the residence of the presidency, of the central comity of the communist party and of some ministries. In the shape of pyramid without a tip (were tested a few domes, idea which was put aside) the palace contains vast lobbies, long corridors, numerous huge halls, and the biggest is called The Union Hall, with a height of sixteen meters and a surface of two thousand two hundred square meters, here lying the biggest chandelier from the palace, with a weight of three tons and seven thousand light bulbs.

The dictator did not speared anything, the interiors being of an uncommon luxury: huge marble stairways, ceilings with ornamental laces, mosaics in special colors, richly carved doors, entire rows of chandeliers and crystal lamps, rugs executed on special orders, furniture on the measure of these beauties and many others. At the Revolution there were finished only a few rooms and the exterior, after this date the works continued up until 1997, when it becomes the Palace of Parliament.

In front of it opens the Constitution Plaza (serves as deployment place for spectacles, parades, celebrations) from which starts then the Union boulevard (former the Victory of the Socialism), which Ceausescu wanted wider than Champs Elysees. The entire artery is strewn with larger or smaller fountains, richly ornamented in stone and of which esthetical level attracted numerous controversies.

# The Old Court

The Old Court, today a complex of fortification ruins, rooms and medieval foundations found between the Victory Path and the Halls street and I. C. Bratianu boulevard is probably one of the most important and old monuments from Bucharest. Often ignored because of the disuse and abandonment state that they suffer from also the entire historical center of Bucharest and of the difficulty of finding them, the ruins from the Old Court have been, for a long time, neglected with the exception of a few archeological researches. In present though, this situation starts to improve along with the start of the renovation and rehabilitation projects of the old Bucharest, and visiting the Old Court re-becomes gradually a fascinating voyage in the rambling and hidden past of Bucharest.

Probably more than the faith of any other monument, the destiny of the stronghold and then of the palace from the Old Court is tightly related of the evolution of Bucharest, from an insignificant village to the capital city of the Romanian Country, and of the lives of some of the most important rulers.

The first constructions are attributed to Mircea cel Batran, and from that moment on the stronghold served as defense point and a core of the extension and development of the settlement Bucharest.

During Vlad Tepes's reign the stronghold becomes the royal residence along with the one from Targoviste and it is consolidated and extended through the craftsmen from Brasov, to which the ruler asked their support in the famous letters toward the people of Brasov. A true medieval castle, the stronghold is in this period a strongly fortified castle and settled on a high hill found on the shore of Dambovita, up until the actual times when the urban development of Bucharest led though at the loss of this aspect.

After it is used as a sole royal residence during Radu cel Frumos, the stronghold passes through the most tumultuous of its moments when it is besieged and conquered by Stefan cel Mare during his involvement in the politic of the Romanian Country in the hope of installing a ruler that was favorable to the anti-Turkish politics. Along with the reign of Basarab the Young follows a long period of constructions and renovations of the Old Court during each reign that grow in size and purpose as Bucharest starts to replace Targoviste as a political center of the Princedom.

Amongst these additions, probably the most important is the church the Old Court or Good Annunciation, raised by Mircea the Shepherd between 1545 and 1554, being since then the coronation place of the rulers of the Romanian Country for the next two centuries. Other notable contributions are made during the rulers Vlad the Monk and Constantin Brancoveanu.

After it was partially destroyed in the fire from 1718 and then in the earthquake from 1738, the complex is rebuilt under the name of The Voivodal Palace, keeping this way its position as royal court and administrative center on the duration of the phanariot rulings and of which ruins constitute most of those that can be visited nowadays. Hereby, if you want to step through the halls through which the steps of numerous rulers passed, now found outdoor, and to step through the still darkened history of Bucharest, the Old Court awaits you along with the museum and the church with the same name.

## The Museum of the Romanian Peasant

The Museum of the Romanian Peasant is one of the most diversified museums from the European family of the Arts Museums and Popular Traditions. The works have started in the year 1912 and ended in 1940, when the building, built in a neo-Romanian style, took the semblance of the actual architecture monument.

The museum is consecrated to the occupations and the traditional artistic sense of the Romanian peasant. It owns approximately ninety thousand Romanian popular art pieces, reunited in collections of ceramic, costumes and fabrics from all the Romanian provinces, popular furniture and hardware, objects accomplished in the carpenter's technique, glass and wood icons, dyed eggs, as well as a little wooden church.

## The Patriarchal Cathedral

The building of the Patriarchy's church was started by the ruler Constantin Serban Basarab in the year 1656, but it will be finished much later by a descendant of his, Radu Leon, just in 1668 and carries name of the "Saint Emperors Constantine and Elena".

After this year, the ruler raises it at the rank of metropolis of the country, and to the hill on which it is placed the people will call The Metropolis' Hill. From the monastic settlements built along with the church, only remains a beautiful and imposing belfry, bricked by Constantin Brancoveanu at the beginning of his reign, in the year 1698. The metropolis is a greater copy of the Neagoe Basarab's church from Curtea de Arges, has a note of simplicity, robustness, balance.

The arcades of the columns of the front are supporting on a thick rock girdle which harmonizes pleasantly with the blind lateral ones; on top, the not too high steeples give an imposing air to the praying dwelling. From the old painting of the church only remained the one from above the entrance door, whereas the one from the inside is from recent date, representing the figures of the ones that built the dwelling or which contributed at its restoration, improvement. The most prized asset of the Metropolis is the silver coffin of the Saint Dimitrie Basarabov in which are resting his remains, a saint much loved by the people, which, as a sign of gratitude, have chosen him the protector of the city.

## The Museum of Bucharest City

The Museum of Bucharest City is a history and art museum found under the tutelage of the Capital City town hall. It is installed in the Sutu Palace situated on the I. C. Bratianu Boulevard, number two, in the center of the capital city. In July 1921, at the proposition of the mayor Gheorghe Gheorghian, the communal council of Bucharest decided to establish the Communal Museum of Bucharest.

The initiative could only be concretized after the capital city town hall put at the disposition of the museum the Moruzi House, a historical building situated on the Victory Path number one hundred and seventeen. The inauguration took place on 22 November 1931, in the presence of the minister-mayor Nicolae Iorga, of the general mayor Dem. I. Dobrescu and of the former mayors Gheorghe Corbescu and Emil Predescu. In 1933 was established the Bucharest City Picture Gallery, as a section of the Communal Museum, which had the headquarters assigned on the Lascar Catargiu Boulevard number seventeen.

The place was donated to the town hall by Ana Urseanu, the wife of the admiral Vasile Urseanu, under the condition that in this place will function both the picture gallery, as well as the Astronomical Observatory.

In 1951, through a violation of the conditions of the Urseanu donation, the picture gallery was evicted from that place. In time, the museum functioned in various locations, most of the places being improper for exhibition activity. Yet, in 1940 in the museum's patrimony were already included four thousand three hundred and thirty pieces. During the Second World War the collections of the museum were kept safe in the village Rosnic. In 1956 the headquarters of the museum was moved into the Sutu Palace from the I. C. Bratianu boulevard number two, where it works up until the present day.

In 1959 the Communal Museum of Bucharest was renamed The History Museum of Bucharest City, which was inaugurated on 23 of January 1959, with the occasion of celebrating a hundred years from the Romanian Princedoms Union. The Art Museum remained a separate entity. In 1984, the Art Museum of Bucharest City and The History Museum unified under the name The History and Art Museum of Bucharest City. In 1999 the name of the museum modified again, taking its actual name of the Museum of Bucharest City.

# The Triumph Arch

The Triumph Arch was built in 1922 from wood and stucco, in the honor of the proclamation of the Union, after the success of the Romanian armies in the First World War, arch which will be replaced with a stone one, the work of the architect Petre Antonescu, between the years 1935-1936.

The southern frontage is beautifully adorned with two medallions in bronze, which picture the faces of the king Ferdinand and the queen Maria, which replace the original ones, destroyed by the communist regime, after the eighties. In their place were applied two great rock flowers, which were removed, after 1989, and the royal faces retook their places.

Above each medallion lies a Victory in relief, works of the sculptors C. Baraski and M. Constantinescu. On the northern frontage, other two medallions bear the sculpted faces of the Manhood and Faith. The Manhood pictures a warrior with a sword, the work of I. Jalea, and Faith pictures a young man with a cross, author C. Baraski.

The victories from above them are executed by the sculptors D. Onofrei and C. Medrea. On the arch rocks of the Triumph Arch are inscribed the battles of the war (Marasesti, Oituz, etcetera), and on the lateral frontages are inscribed the proclamations of the king Ferdinand toward the people when the country went into war and the one from Alba Iulia with the occasion of the coronation.

# Victoria Palace

The Victoria Palace is the work of the professor Duiliu Marcu (1885-1966), a student of the Superior Architecture School from Bucharest (1906) and then of Ecole de Beaux-Arts from Paris (diplomat in 1912).

After a first period of activity, situated at the beginning in the formulas of the French academism, then in the ones of the neo-Romanian style, Duiliu Marcu joined in the thirties to the modern current, becoming one of its main protagonists from Romania.

Both the interiors and the frontages of the Victoria Palace illustrate the preoccupation to keep the classical fundament and to make to appear the idea of modern simplicity. In the present here lies the headquarters of the Govern of Romania.

# The National Village Museum "Dimitrie Gusti"

In the spring of the year 1936 was founded the Museum of the Romanian Village, a collective creation of the Romanian Sociological School, founded and leaded by professor Dimitrie Gusti. The one that first thought on constituting a collection of popular art, of the types of peasantry homes and presenting them in exhibitions was the writer Al. Odobescu, long time ago. At its opening, the museum contained a surface of five hectares and only thirty peasant houses, characteristic for various areas of the country. At their placement took part culture people, specialists, one thousand and one hundred workers of various occupations and one hundred and thirty popular craftsmen from the villages of the selected houses. All over the years, the surface of the museum grew up to about fifteen hectares, and the number of constructions placed overcomes the number three hundred; from these over four hectares are equipped with all that is necessary for a peasantry household (workshops, annex constructions, churches etcetera).

In 1977 it gained the name the Village Museum and of Popular Art through the merger with the Museum of Popular Art. After the Revolution, in March 1990, they divided again, the first becoming the Village Museum, and the second the Museum of the Romanian Peasant. Placed on a side of the Herastrau Park in parallel with Kiseleff driveway, the Village Museum, through its size, becomes the greatest outdoor museum from Europe, which attracts through its beauty numerous foreign tourists, but also people from Bucharest that are eager to take a walk.

# The Herastrau Park

Herastrau Park is the greatest park from Bucharest and the greatest park found inside a town from Europe. It has a surface of one hundred and ten hectares and spreads on the two shores of the lake Herastrau. The layout of the park started in the year 136 according to the projects of the architects Emil Pinard and Frederich Rebhun, the alleys being designed by the architect Octav Dobrescu.

It contains a rich variety of trees, formed of willows, poplars, ash, linden and maple. On the alleys of the park are placed statues of important characters from the national and universal culture. The initial name was The Carol the Second Park, and when the communist regime came to power, the name was changed into the Iosif Vissarionovici Stalin Park. In the year 1948 it received the name of Herastrau Park, and in 1951, gained the actual form. In park lies The Village Museum, EspoFlora, the Japanese Garden, The Island of the Roses, but also fields and sportive bases, restaurants and a pier from where it can be taken rides with the boat or the ship. Also in the perimeter of the park lies the Elisabeta Palace, realized between the years 1936 and 1937, in Moorish-Spanish style. It carries the name of Princess Elisabeta, the ex queen of Greece and a sister of the king Carol. In the present it belongs to the Royal House of Romania.

## The Youth Park

Localized in the south of Bucharest, in the vicinity of Berceni neighborhood, of the Vacaresti Lake and Carol Park, the Youth is the third park in size from the capital city, occupying a surface of eighty hectares. If Herastrau Park can take pride in numerous activities which cover all the age categories, and the IOR Park offers long promenades in a quiet and invigorating environment, the Youth Park is, in return, a park destined for children, having numerous playgrounds, wide alleys, fair attractions and sportive facilities. Built from 1965 to 1974, the Youth is the creation of the architect Valentin Donose, of which mission was setting a green space for "the recreation and rest of the working class" from the southern areas of Bucharest, of which extension and development took place in the same period.

Since then and until today the park suffered few modifications and numerous periods of neglecting. Recently though, were started numerous redevelopment and modernization projects which managed to refresh the park by cleaning the lake, creating floral gardens and new playgrounds, especially in the south-eastern area called now the Children's Park.

The two main entrances of the park are the ones found in front of the Constantin Brancoveanu subway station, close to which is found the area called the Children's Town with numerous attractions of fairs amongst which a rollercoaster, bumper cars, mechanical vehicles, skills contents and the steam train which goes up to nearby the lake; and the one found in front of Youth subway station, from which it can be entered in the northern part of the park equipped with wide alleys, playgrounds and steep hills, used as slide during winter. In the interior of the park lies the lake with the same name, of which sinuous shores are ideal for meditation and rest, on the benches, on green and steep lawns or on one of the two islands.

Other points of interest are: -the Polyvalent Hall dedicated to sports, - the Children's Palace, the place of numerous fairs, concerts and other cultural events, -the area from the back of the Polyvalent Hall, which presents a very great surface dedicated to the bicycle tracks and roller skates, as well as the entrance in the Bellu cemetery, in which popular personalities are buried, such as: Ion Luca Caragiale, Mihai Eminescu, Henri Coanda, Nicolae Iorga, Aurel Vlaicu etcetera. As the name suggests, the Youth Park is an ideal place for children and young, offering them an ideal playground and relaxation place, away from the dust and crowd from the center, and easily accessible through the subway stations from the second line.

# The Museum of Romanian Literature

Situated on Dacia boulevard number twelve, the National Museum of Romanian Literature shelters an authentic literary thesaurus formed from manuscripts, books, personal objects, art objects, photos, audio-video recordings. These reproduce into an image concentrated metaphorical the depth, the complexity and ineffable beauty of the Romanian literature. The actual permanent exhibition combines the classical methods of exposure with last generation technologies, interactive.

The systems of "touchscreen" type complete the historical-documentary information present in the exhibition. This way, the visitors can interact with the work of the Romanian writers through the recitation of several known actors, film adaptations and theatrical adaptations. Along with the exhibitions with permanent and itinerant character, the museum of the Romanian literature hosts numerous other presences of the same kind, but limited as exposing period. These have the purpose to accompany or create the surrounding of other cultural manifestations, such as book presentations, thematic debates, conferences, events (the night of the museums, the Bucharest days, the day of the open gates).

## The Botanic Garden

Localized in the center of the city, in the immediate vicinity of the Cotroceni Palace, the Botanic Garden is probably one of the most beautiful places from Bucharest, delighting its visitors with over ten thousand plant species: from tall trees to the tiniest flowers, and beside the role to delight its visitors, the garden continues to be an ideal background for the botanical scientific studies and educating the population by displaying the diversity of the vegetal world and the problems that it confronts with, in the interactions with the human. A walk through the Botanic Garden becomes this way a journey in the plants' universe which is as instructive as it is relaxing.

After the first botanic garden, found near the Carol Davila Faculty of Medicine and finished in 1860, to make place for a park destined exclusively for the royal family, it was demolished, the academician and exceptional botanist Dimitrie Brandza laid consistent efforts to create a new place dedicated to the studies and botanical education. These efforts materialized eventually in 1884 when it started the constructions on the actual place of the garden, and in 1994 the garden received the honorary name of the one that fought for its existence, being called: the "Dimitrie Brandza" Botanic Garden of the University of Bucharest. Since then and up until today, the garden passed through numerous difficult moments, the first even in the following year of its opening, in 1892, being confronted with the massive floods which devastated the capital city, then in the First World War when it is used by the German troupes of occupation, in 1932 when it is taken from the administration of the University of Bucharest and transformed into a simple park, and in 1944 when it is bombarded by the English-American planes. In 1954, it returns under the administration of the University, and since then the plant collections and specimens were restored, reaching again the number from the early times. Today the Botanical Garden can pride with a surface of 17.5 hectares, from which 0.4 are occupied by a green house which recreates the equatorial and tropical environment, with a museum in which are exposed the five hundred thousand plants for the herbarium, as well as stuffed animals specific to the environments found in Romania, and a multitude of plants from all the existent types, attended and adapted to survive and thrive in the temperate continental climate of Bucharest.

An ideal green space both for tourists as well as for specialists, the Botanical Garden remains one of the oldest "outdoor monuments" of Bucharest, which continues to delight and fascinate its visitors even after more than a century full of adventures passed since its establishment. Surely, it is an example which shows us that beautiful places can survive in Bucharest despite all the calamities that can happen and the political changes that might occur.

# III. The Weather in Bucharest

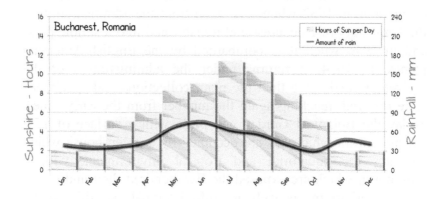

## The Climate

Bucharest has a continental climate, characterized through warm summers, dry and cold winters.

Because of its position on the Romanian Plain, during winter it can appear very strong winds, but most of the air currents lose their intensity because of the urbanization degree. The temperatures from during the winter are often below zero degrees Celsius, very rare they can get below minus ten degrees Celsius.

In the summer, the medium temperature is twenty three degrees Celsius (the average for July and August), but it can climb even to thirty five-forty degrees Celsius in the middle of the summer in the center of the city. Even though during the summer the average of the precipitations and humidity is low, it can appear, sporadically, strong storms, often violent. During spring and fall, the temperatures vary between eighteen-twenty two degrees Celsius, and the precipitation in this period tends to be more elevated than during summer, with more frequent rains, but also more gentle.

| Month | Average solar light (hours) | Temperature | | | | Discomfort due to the heat and humidity | Relative humidity | | The average of the precipitations (mm) | Very humid days (+0.25 mm) |
| | | Average | | Recordings | | | | | | |
| | | Min | Max | Min | Max | | AM | PM | | |
| Jan | 2 | -7 | 1 | -32 | 16 | - | 87 | - | 46 | 11 |
| Feb | 3 | -5 | 4 | -26 | 20 | - | 84 | - | 26 | 9 |
| Mar | 5 | -1 | 10 | -19 | 29 | - | 73 | - | 28 | 9 |
| Apr | 6 | 5 | 18 | -4 | 32 | - | 63 | - | 59 | 11 |
| May | 8 | 10 | 23 | 0 | 37 | Moderate | 63 | - | 77 | 13 |
| Jun | 9 | 14 | 27 | 5 | 37 | Medium | 62 | - | 121 | 12 |
| Jul | 11 | 16 | 30 | 8 | 39 | Medium | 58 | - | 53 | 10 |
| Aug | 10 | 15 | 30 | 7 | 41 | Medium | 59 | - | 45 | 7 |
| Sep | 8 | 11 | 25 | 0 | 39 | Moderate | 63 | - | 45 | 5 |
| Oct | 5 | 6 | 18 | -6 | 35 | - | 73 | - | 29 | 7 |
| Nov | 2 | 2 | 10 | -14 | 24 | - | 85 | - | 36 | 12 |
| Dec | 2 | -3 | 4 | -23 | 18 | - | 89 | - | 27 | 10 |

# IV. The Transit

## Bucharest Metro

In this moment the transportation network stretches on 69.25 kilometers of double way, there are four highways with fifty one stations, and the average distance between two stations is one and a half kilometer.

**RATB**

In 1871 establishes the first "Romanian Society of Tramcars", on the streets of Bucharest being seen the first tramcars pulled by horses. In 1990 the Enterprise of Transport Bucharest (ETB) transforms into the Autonomous Overhead of Transport Bucharest (RATB), through the Decision of the Bucharest City's City Hall. It is elaborated a new strategy regarding the functioning and development of the public transportation of the surface of Bucharest. It takes place the detachment of the taxi units and maxi-taxi of RATB.

# Night buses:

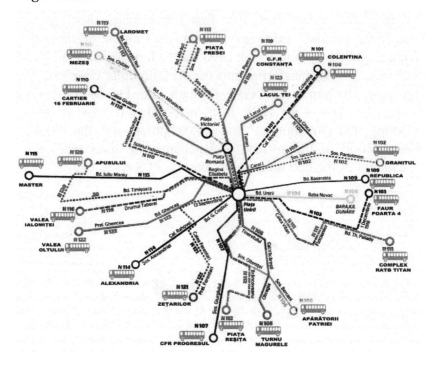

# V. Statistics About Bucharest

## Population
**Inhabitants:** 1.926.334

**Density:** 8.510 inhabitants /square kilometer

| Nationality | Percentage |
|---|---|
| Romanians | 96,9 |
| Gipsies | 1,4 |
| Hungarians | 0,3 |
| Jews | 0,1 |
| Turks | 0,1 |
| Chinese | 0,1 |

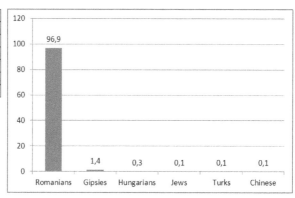

| Religion | Percentage |
|---|---|
| Ortodox | 96,1 |
| Catholics | 1,2 |
| Islamics | 0,5 |
| Greek-Catholics | 0,4 |
| Other religions | 1,8 |

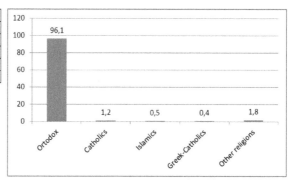

## Geographical Coordinates

**Latitude:** 44 degrees 24 minutes 49 seconds

**Longitude:** 26 degrees05minutes48seconds

**Altitude:** sixty-ninety meters above sea level

**Surface:** two hundred and twenty eight square kilometers (0.8% from the surface of Romania, from which the built surface is seventy percent).

**Surface with the urban area:** two hundred and eighty five square kilometers.

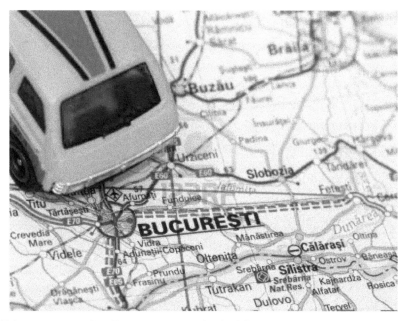

**Distances to the European capital cities:**

385 kilometers-Sofia

567 kilometers-Belgrade

1626  kilometers- Berlin

1044 kilometer- Vienna

549 kilometers- Athens

1379 kilometers-Rome

3890 kilometers-Lisboan

2302 kilometers-Madrid

2460 kilometers-Andorra la Vela

1947 kilometers-Luxembourg

2119 km-Brussels

2154 km-Amsterdam

2465 km-London

2956 km-Dublin

1856 km-Monaco

3677 km-Reykjavik

2165 km- Oslo

1577 km-Stockholm

2071 km-Helsinki

1748 km-Copenhagen

2424 km-Moscow

916 km-Kiev

1334 km-Minsk

448 km-Chisinau

810 km-Podgorica

606 km-Skopje

879 km-Tirana

1203 km-Nicosia

1398 km-La Valletta

1309 km-San Marino

1379 km-Vatican

813 km-Sarajevo

963 km-Zagreb

1320 km-Prague

2066 km-Tallinn

802 km-Budapest

1755 km-Riga

1638 km-Vaduz

1399 km-Vilnius

1169 km-Warsaw

2223 km-Paris

994 km-Bratislava

1098 km-Ljubljana

1840 km-Berne

# VI. The history of Bucharest

Trying to redact a history of Bucharest is a very difficult thing to do. First of all you must get used to the idea that you will never manage to encompass all.

Despite jibing with the history of this city by certain contemporaries, Bucharest has, no doubt, a very rich history in events and names. There are a thousand experiences from international treaties up to slum fights which remained written and then noticed by historians. What is truly important? Which were the events that really changed the evolution of Bucharest from small scattered settlements to the capital city of Romania from today? These are questions to which numerous historians tried to answer.

This article is my attempt to resume a story which might fill (and it did) entire volumes, the story of a city which did not influenced the world such as Rome and Athens, which was little known by anyone else beside its inhabitants (and which is pretty obscure even nowadays), which did not risen from ranks as a center of politics from the beginnings of its existence, such as Paris and London did, but just in the last centuries. It is still the story of a city which always made a strong impression to those that inhabited it or which only passed by and which is full of overthrows of situations, tragedies and heroic battles. What you will read in the following you probably already knew, but I do not think this will stop you from reading this synopsis. So let us go from the beginning…

### Prehistory and Antiquity

The first historical mentions about Bucharest come from the fourteenth century, but this does not mean that the first inhabitants date from that period. No doubt, the area on which nowadays lies the capital city of Romania was populated since Prehistory. The first historiographic proofs date from the late Paleolithic (the first Stone Age, which remarks through simple tools and temporary settlements of reduced dimensions). Then follows the artifacts from Mesolithic, which were also replaced by the ones originated from the Neolithic. Only starting now we talk about real art objects and some sophisticated which belong to the Glina and Gumelnita cultures, of which area included vast areas from the Balkans.

Immediately with the start of the Bronze Age also appears the Tei culture, an original form specific exclusively to the Ilfov area derived probably from the Glina culture. Now that we have certain knowledge about the cultures that mastered the area, let us try to figure out how did Bucharest looked like, or at least the space on which it will be built on, in this period. All over the shores of Dambovita stretched the Vlasiei Woods, of which wild and green assembly was interrupted by the areas on which it was already started cultivating the wheat, and which were going to impress so much the Macedonians of Alexander the Great a few centuries later. Strewn through these plains of nature were found numerous little villages often formed of primitive huts, and rarely constructions which could have remind of houses, always built of wood and mud.

These small settlements had a temporary character, being abandoned according to the cycle of transhumance, in which the inhabitants concerned themselves with hunting, fishing and rarely agriculture. Most of these settlements seem to have been concentrated in the outskirts areas such as: Colentina, Herastrau, Tei, Pantelimon, Popesti-Leordeni etcetera, but this thing can be put on the fact that in the central areas could not be attempted archeological researches. It is very likely for the center to have been rich in these kinds of settlements, especially if we bear in mind the numerous tools discovered that were used for fishing, which would have definitely been used on the shores of Dambovita. In the dacic period this situation continues to be mostly unchanged.

The area of Bucharest is nothing else than a point on the route of the shepherds that carry their sheep year after year from the mountain to the plain, away from the center of the dacic power Transylvania, having nothing interesting to offer to the dace kings and chieftains. Neither the Romans were interested on the region. In the Roman period, the Bucharest territory continued to be a no man land, scoured and lived sometimes by shepherds, avoided by the numerous barbarian people which were permanently looking for rich preys, and occasionally stepped by the Roman or Byzantine troupes which were trying to restore the imperial control in the abandoned Dacia, such was the case of the troupes of Constantine the Great and Justinian.

Despite this statute of weekly populated territory and basically savage, it have been discovered even here traces of the Romanization, such as the coins discovered in the areas Giulesti, Tei and Radu-Voda. There also exists a toponimic proof of the period of establishment of the slaves in that area, through the name from nowadays: Snagov, Chiajna, Glina and Colentina.

**The Middle Age**

According to tradition, Bucharest has taken its name from the shepherd Bucur, of which house, the first from the city, stayed on the nowadays place of the Bucur's Church. Either we believe this legend or not, we previously saw that since Prehistory, the today capital city represented an important point on the route of the transhumance, so it is not too difficult to imagine that some of these shepherds started to establish permanent households in the area, which gradually started to gain the aspect of a village.

Also, during the reign of Vladislav Vlaicu appears a mention of the village of Dambovita, which could be Bucharest. No matter if this is the case or not, once with the reign of Mircea cel Batran is built for the first time "the stronghold on Dambovita", which was situated on the place in which today we find the ruins from the Old Court. This stronghold was nothing else than a wooden fort, surrounded by a tall palisade and a few houses made also from wood, which probably were originated in the village that was previous to the fortifications. In the context in which Mircea was building Giurgiu as a center of his power, to be closer to the territories found on south of the Danube where he was engaged in the civil war from the Ottoman Empire, triggered at the death of Bayazid, Bucharest served as an intermediary fortified point between the capital city from Targoviste and Mircea's new center of power from Giurgiu. Under the following rullers Giurgiu will be lost to the Turks, the capital city will be established at Targoviste to be as close as possible to Ardeal and as far as possible to the Ottoman territories from below the Danube, and the military importance of Bucharest drops considerably.

Despite this fact, the necessary impulse for the development has been given. Under the form of "the stronghold on Dambovita", the locality is a military village, in which predominate the smithies, the forges, the barracks and the wooden pillars, and this situation will be maintained until the reign of Vlad Tepes. Within his aggressive politics and his numerous campaigns and expeditions to south of Danube, Vlad needed a new ruling place closer to Danube than Targoviste. So he chooses to make from the old stronghold of Mircea cel Batran a new capital city for the Romanian Country.

In the famous letters toward the inhabitants of Brasov he asks, amongst others, to send handymen which will transform the old wooden fort into a real castle. This represents the second impulse from the history of the city which puts it on a clear progress trajectory, which could not be derailed despite the numerous disasters through which the city had to pass, from epidemics to plague, to sieges and destructions. In the following years, the city will develop into a very fast rhythm, especially because of the numerous churches that were going to be built both by rulers and the important lordly families.

Owning broad estates which included: vineyards, agricultural lands and grass, the churches and the monasteries have built the core around which the merchants and the craftsmen were attracted, of which workshops, households and stores have led to the gradual extension of the city. Their presence also meant the strong development of the commerce, making the city more and more difficult to ignore for the rulers. Regarding the status of capital city, the fifteenth and sixteenth centuries remarked through the permanent competition between Bucharest, Targoviste and Curtea de Arges for the honor to be the place of the ruler. Generally the branch of Draculestians, the descendants of Vlad Tepes, have always inclined toward Bucharest, while the more direct branch of the Basarabs tended toward Curtea de Arges and then toward Targoviste, even though there are individual exceptions in both dynasties. There is also a turbid period in which the dynastic fights and the wars with the Ottomans make the stronghold to be under siege many times. Amongst sieges and robberies are counted the conquest of the city by Stefan cel Mare, to remove Radu cel Frumos from power, the brother of Vlad Tepes, which was applying a politic aligned to Turkey, the raids of the tartars from the sixteenth century, the rejected siege of the Transylvanian-Hungarian forces of the ruler Nicholas and, the most devastating from all, the Turkish occupation of the forces of Sinan Pasha in the context of the fights with Mihai Viteazul. Even though during this occupation the city was almost completely scorched, only a year later almost everything was rebuilt.

Up until the phanariot rulings have come, Bucharest could no longer be changed with Targoviste, it has become already a too great economical and religious center. Constantin Brancoveanu had no other choice than to build the palace from

Mogosoaia as a center of his court, even though he would have preferred to rule from Targoviste. As a city, Bucharest was at that time a vast alternation of crowded houses and wide spaces destined for agriculture, and even areas that were still occupied by the Vlasiei Woods, reason for which establishing the borders of the city and its real denizens number was a very difficult task.

### The Phanariot Period

Despite the general fatal character of the phanariot rulings, for Bucharest, this period was one of flourish and development. Under the guidance of some rulers such as Nicolae Mavrocordat and Alexandru Ipsilanti, are placed the first pavements, appear the first schools and universities from Bucharest and it starts the period of extension of the urban concentrations and the limitation of the estates destined for agriculture, which will be ended only toward the start of the twentieth century. Also in these decades it start to appear the slums of which organization was similar to the one from Constantinople and which takes to the concentration of certain social categories or ethnic groups and cults in certain neighborhoods. In this period we have a slum of Catholics, one of the Jews, another for the Armenians, of the undertakers, of the butchers etcetera. Even though the membership to these slums is not exclusivist, for example it could have been existed carpenters in the slum dedicated to the butchers, most of the inhabitants of a slum have as a main source of activity the one of that slum.

Concomitant with the slums it start to appear the first forms of bucharestian conscience, under the form of riots and revolts which often were overthrowing the ruler and were forcing the Gate to assign a new one, as well as through the growing rivalries between the main lordly families, similar, rather, to the fights from today amongst the sportive galleries.

72

Even though at this date the city was mostly covered by mud, flooded by Dambovita and full of vineyards and orchards, this did not stopped the lords and the merchants with aspirations to wear rich clothes, in strident colors, into a clothing style which borrowed generously both from the Orient and the Occident, with numerous jewelries as accessories, and to walk in sumptuously ornated calashes and carriages, sometimes pulled by deer, such is the case of the ruler Nicolae Mavroghen. Grace to this cosmopolite assembly, which was mixing into the background along with the most lifelike images of poverty, Bucharest starts to gain that unique aspect, through which it imposes into the memory of the foreign travelers, as the border point between the European influences and the Asian ones, and the fusion and exchange place between the two cultures.

### The Local Rulings and the Organic Regulation

The restoration of the local rulings, as a consequence of the riot of Tudor Vladimirescu from 1821, which was going to name the neighborhood Drumul Taberei, as a place of establishment for the revolutionists camp, will not have a major effect over the city.

The demographic growth, the extension of the modernization projects, the accentuation of the urbanization and the cultural life will continue relentless in the nineteenth century as well, despite de fires, the plagues and earthquakes which haunted the city in this period. Even though Bucharest was already occupied a few times by the Austrian and Russian troupes, as a consequence of the numerous wars from the three empires, only now they will have a visible effect over the city, more exactly the Russian occupation of the general Kiseleff from 1829 until 1834. Along the establishment of the Organic Regulation, known today as being the first example of constitution in Romania, Pavel Kiselyov, on his Russian name, was probably the first ruler of the city that started an ample process of modernization.

Amongst the realizations of his administration are the following: making exact censes, mapping and defining vastness of the properties, the buildings and the city itself, creating and extending the city's sewerage, the paving for the first time the streets with cubic stone, and not with wooden plaques such was the case during the phanariot rulings, and which proved its inefficiency during rains, a thing written in the famous novel of Nicolae Filimon, "The old and new upstarts", the construction of public fountains, bringing to the standard of the age the firemen service, the drainage of the swampy areas from close by Dambovita and creating the boulevards: Calea Dorobantilor and the Kiseleff driveway.

Despite these ample projects of modernization and beautification, the strong material and cultural contrast appeared in the age of the phanariots continues to be omnipresent and continues to be remarked by foreign travelers such as the French Marc Girardin. Still, the projects of Kiseleff, as well as of the following rulers managed to give in the end a true urban aspect to the city. If until then the capital city could have been easily seen as an over-extended and fragmented village, now it really looks like an European city, having structured streets, multiple floors buildings and clearly defined townsman areas.

Another marking novelty appeared in this period is the press and the literary cenacles. Under the rulers from the Ghica and Bibescu families, the newspapers and even literary magazines will start to gain popularity, having a growing edition. Even though their golden age will only start along with the ruling of Cuza, these publications disclose their importance especially during the event from 1848, in which they joined most of the citizens around the riot, along with the actions and speeches done by Ion Heliade Radulescu, Nicolae Balcescu etcetera.

## The Small Paris

The century passed between 1859 and 1946 was going to be the most flourishing for Bucharest. Became the capital city of the entire Romania as a consequence of the double election of Alexandru Ioan Cuza, the city was going to pass through a real economical, demographic and cultural boom. On an economical plan it is the period in which the great factories of the city will be opened, which was covering consumption objects such as: cigarettes, bier, soaps, candles, textiles and even heavy machineries and planes. In the same time the city serves as an important commercial center, attracting the businessmen and magnates from all Europe and even from the United States.

These massive business and financial opportunities have led to the progressive apparition of the native bourgeoisie represented both by the small merchandisers and the great industrialists and magnates, which were going to replace the former lords and priests as the most important and powerful class from the city. Also now will grow in number the workers' class, attracted by the opportunity presented by the new factories. Under the impulse of the demographic growth and the apparition of a new economical life which no longer relied on agriculture, the urbanization process is finished. Are built an impressive number of buildings of all kinds, belonging to some extremely various architectural styles and the last green spaces disappear or are transformed into parks. The coffee shops, the boutiques, the window shops, even the houses with a balcony appear in this period and start to be a part of the life of the city.

This way, the new city with wide streets, with tramcars pulled by horses, with buildings of a few floors found close by the gardens rich with trees of various types, is named by its visitors "The Small Paris", being still a city of contrasts and scandals, but at the same time, an unique picture, a mix of cultures and at the same time an original creation itself. To complete this cultural picture, it must also be mentioned the cenacles, the literary publications and the great writers of Romania which passed through Bucharest in a moment of their life, if not living their entire life in it. From the romantic Mihai Eminescu, to the realists Liviu Rebreanu and Camil Petrescu, up to the modernists Tudor Arghezi and Lucian Blaga, all have passed through Bucharest and were influenced by it more or less. Some of them transposed the city in their works, such as Mateiu Caragiale in his definitive novel and the short works of his arch-known father, the poems of Alexanndru Macedonski and George Bacovia, the townsman novels of Camil Petrescu, Hortensia Papadat-Bengescu and Mihail Sebastian and the balzacian works of George Calinescu. Either they watch in disgust the urban crowd or are impressed by its world, they all offer us a sample of the glory period of the city.

Also in this period the Bucharest will be occupied by the German troupes in the First World War, will be struck by numerous earthquakes and fires, will be the scene of numerous revolts and riots, from the conspiracy to remove Cuza, up to the coup d'état against the Antonescu regime, and will be bombarded by the English-American allies and then by the former German allies during the Second World War. But despite all these disasters, the life and the progress continued as they did in the past, the city still attracting new denizens from simple workers to artistic geniuses.

## The Communist Period

About the demolishes and the reorganization process of Bucharest according to the lines of the socialist realism we will not be talking too much. This subject was debated enough to fill the reading of a lifetime, and the subject itself is one pretty painful and fresh in the memory of many of us.

Shortly, the communist Bucharest characterized through raising new neighborhoods of residential blocks, specific for the communist countries, the placement of statues with the purpose of the glorification of the doctrines and leaders, the demolishment of churches and old buildings which were sitting in the way of the new urban plan, the creation of cyclopean plants and factories toward the margin of the city etcetera.

Therefore, without insisting furthermore, in this period many of the elements that constituted the charm and style of the "Small Paris" have been lost forever. Let us try in return to see the more positive accomplishments made in those years, because yes, there have been this kind of constructions and projects. Amongst these we can remind: the subway, the fastest and more efficient mean of transportation from the Bucharest suffocated of traffic; the House of People, which even though is blasphemed by many for the costs and the demolishes made in its name, is beyond debate one of the most important monuments from the entire Romania; the parks and green spaces from the suburbia, such as Youth and IOR; paving the streets and the sidewalks, of which utility in transportation and the resilience to the nature's caprices cannot be denied.

With the risk of seeming pathetic, I must say that any dark moment from history has its good parts, if you are willing to look carefully, and if the communist period has brought any progress in the city, then these were the efficiency of the transportation system, of sewerage and electricity. The communist Bucharest was a safer city, more quiet and with better facilities than the inter-war Bucharest, in the same time though it was an uglier city, almost completely grey, which has lost its magic and the puff that made it so miraculous to the strangers.

### After the Revolution

After the Revolution from 89, probably the greatest riot from the many that Bucharest has seen before, it has been attempted to restore the idea of "Small Paris", but the legacy left by the communism cannot be erased or masked. Instead of demolishes and disuses, it should be found a method through which the socialist remains, some very great and omnipresent remains, to be integrated in the bigger picture of a city, which proved us after many centuries that it can adapt and to thrive in any historical and political situation, no matter how harsh. I think that it is too early to identify the direction of evolution of Bucharest, in this new context, but until now two phenomena seem consolidated:

1) the abandonment of the factories and the great complexes from the communist period, and

2) the extension in an almost supersonic rhythm of the malls, supermarkets and other massive similar commercial complexes, both in the suburbs and in the areas close to the center. The history of this period of Bucharest is still been written, and maybe in a few decades we will be able to say that it also had something unique. Until then I propose to look at the future optimistic.

# VII. Useful Information

**Shopping in Bucharest**

**AFI Palace Cotroceni**
Address: Bd. Vasile Milea, no. 4
Phone: 031.425.75.10
Internet: www.aficotroceni.ro

**Baneasa Shopping City**
Address: Str. C.A.Rosetti, no. 5
Phone: 021.310.01.00
Internet: www.baneasa.ro

**Bucuresti Mall**
Address: Calea Vitan, no. 55-59
Phone: 021.327.67.00/021.327.61.02/021.327.61.00
Internet: www.bucurestimall.com.ro

## Militari Shopping Center

Address: Bd. Iuliu Maniu, no. 536-560

Phone: 021.380.87.82/0752.10.10.22

Internet: www.militari-shopping.ro

## Plaza Romania

Address: Bd. Timisoara, no. 26

Phone: 021.407.84.75/021.407.84.83

Internet: www.plazaromania.ro

## Sun Plaza

Address: Calea Vacaresti, no. 391

Internet: www.sunplaza.ro

## Unirea Shopping Center

Address: Piata Unirii, no. 1

Phone: 021.30.30.208/021.30.30.307

Internet: www.unireashop.ro

## Rent A Car in Bucharest

## Active

Address: Str. Arhitect Louis Blanc, no.2, Bloc I1

Phone: 231.44.89 / 0727.644.644

Internet: www.active-rentacar.ro

**Amd Motors**

Phone: 461.06.01 / 0722.335.935 / 0741.906.749

Internet: www.amdmotors.ro

**Carbiz**

Address: Str. Stanislau Cihovsky

Phone: 0788 CARBIZ / 0723 565 353 / 0722 453 893

Internet: www.carbiz.ro

**Delta Rentals**

Address: Bd. Tineretului, no. 3

Phone: 320.88.21 / 0723.349.930

Internet: www.bucharest-rentacar.ro

**E-Motion**

Address: Str. Izvor, no. 78.

Phone: 031 4011.307 / 031 4011.998

Internet: www.rent-a-car-romania.com

**Emerald Automobile**

Phone: 430.46.09 / 0726.723.723

Internet: www.emerald-auto.ro

**EuroCars**

Address: Bd. Unirii, no. 21

Phone: 0727.373.799 / 0744.823.488

Internet: www.eurocars.ro

**Thrifty Car Rental Romania**

Address: Pta. Montreal, nr 10 (World Trade Center, Intrarea. F, 2.28) / Aeroport Henri Coanda (Otopeni) / Aeroport Baneasa

Phone: 319.04.32 / 201.46.68 / 230.40.56

Internet: www.thrifty.ro

**Useful Phone Numbers in Bucharest**

**112 - emergency number**

Phone: 112

Internet: www.112.ro

Details: The number 112 is a fast way to communicate with the emergency dispatch (Police, Fire Squad, Ambulance) during an emergency.

The 112 service operates on a national level in all phone networks.

**Baneasa Airport**

Phone: 021-232.00.20

Internet: www.baneasa-airport.ro

**Otopeni Airport**

Phone: 021-204.10.00/021-201.40.00

Internet: www.otp-airport.ro

**Weather Information**

Phone: 021-9591

**SNCFR  Information (Trains timetable)**

Phone: 021-9521

**TAROM  Information**

Phone: 021-9361

**RATB  Information (buses and trams)**

Phone: 021-9391

**Exact Time**

Phone: 021-958

Internet: www.romtelecom.ro/personal/voce/serviciul-ora-exacta/

Price: 0,119 euro/min

**Consumer Protection Service**

Phone: 0800.080.999 / 021-312.12.75

Internet: www.anpc.gov.ro

Lightning Source UK Ltd.
Milton Keynes UK
UKHW02f1552160618
324300UK00009B/74/P